GR/ FOS

INTO
THE
PYRAMID

Mark Foster
and
Phillip Burrows

'**S**top!
Stop! There's the shop.
It's there,' says Alberta. The car stops.

Alberta is Anna's mother and they are on holiday in Egypt. Alberta is an actress. Every year she makes a new film. But today, she wants a haircut. She has a lot of haircuts.

The driver gets out of the car and opens the door for Alberta. 'Good-bye, Anna. Meet me at the hotel in three hours,' Alberta says.

'Quick, you're late. Bye, Mother.' says Anna.

'Look after Lucretia.' There is a cat in the car. Alberta puts her hand on the cat. 'Be a good girl, Lucretia,' she says to the cat.

- Alberta goes into a shop. What is its name?

Hamid, the driver, closes the door. 'Where are we going now?' he asks Anna.

'Oh, I don't know,' she replies. 'I don't like Egypt. It's too hot and there is nothing to do.'

'Let's go to the market. It's not hot there,' says Hamid.

He drives Anna to the market. Lucretia wants to get out of the car. She can see fish and she is hungry. Anna puts a lead on Lucretia and they go into the market.

There are a lot of people. Lucretia pulls on the lead and Anna is soon in the middle of the market. There are people selling carpets and there are people selling food. Anna and Lucretia see someone selling dogs. Lucretia does not like dogs. Suddenly Anna thinks: 'I'm lost! I must get out of the market. But how?'

- The market is very busy.
  Can you see Lucretia?

Lucretia does not like the market because she is afraid of the dogs. She runs away. She knows which way to go and Anna follows her out of the market.

'Good girl, Lucretia,' Anna tells her.

'Let's get in the car. I'd like to see the pyramids. Would you?' Anna asks Lucretia.

The cat says: 'Meow.'

Lucretia and Anna get in the car. They ask Hamid to drive to the pyramids. There are a lot of cars on the roads and it takes a long time to get there.

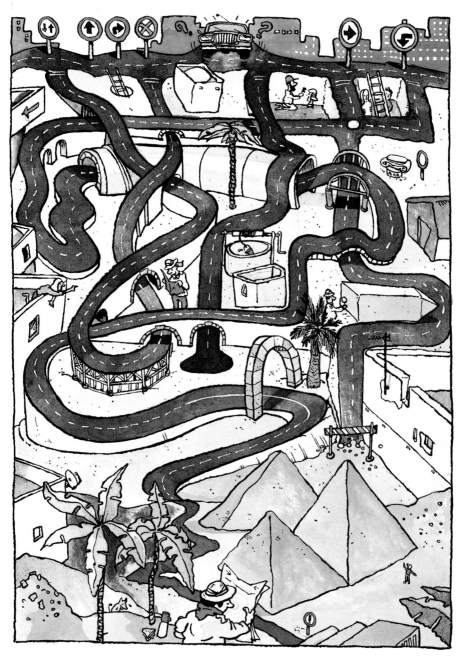

• How do Anna and Lucretia get to the pyramids?

At the pyramids, Anna and Lucretia get out of the car. The pyramids are very beautiful. Anna says: 'They're very old – and very strange, too! What do you think, Lucretia?'

Lucretia is quiet.

'What are you looking at, cat?' says Anna. Lucretia is looking at one of the pyramids. There are a lot of people and a film camera. Anna sees a white cat there, and Lucretia is looking at it.

They walk to the pyramid. 'This is exciting,' thinks Anna.

There are big lights around the pyramid – and there are a lot of tins of cat food. A man is asking people to do things. The film is an advertisement and the man is the director. He wants the white cat to sit by the pyramid, but the cat walks away. The director gets angry.

'The cat's not doing what I want. Why not?' he asks. A woman in a red dress picks up the cat. 'My cat's tired,' says the woman. 'He's very hot.'

'I'm hot and tired, too,' says the director. He walks to his chair. He wants to sit down but he can't. 'Ahhhgggg,' he says.

• The director cannot sit in his chair. Why not?

Anna watches the director. He looks at Anna. He sees Lucretia and smiles.

'Hello,' he says.

'Hello,' says Anna.

'Meow,' says Lucretia.

The director says to Anna, 'Your cat's beautiful. Does she want to be in my advertisement?' He says to Lucretia, 'Would you like to be in my advertisement?'

Lucretia says 'Meow' again.

Anna is very happy. 'Yes,' she says. 'Thank you. We'd like that.'

The director puts a collar on Lucretia. On the collar are the words 'Top Cat'. Anna watches as the director picks up Lucretia. He puts her in front of the camera.

Suddenly the director claps his hands: 'Listen to me, please. I want the short man to stand by the pyramid. I want the tall woman to stand by the car. And I want the cat to stand by the cat food.'

• Are the people in the right places?

The director tells everybody what to do. The short man and the tall woman must sing a song. At the end of the song Lucretia must say 'meow'. Then she must eat some cat food.

Lucretia is very good. She says 'meow' and eats the food. Anna claps excitedly. The director wants them to do it again. And again. And again.

Lucretia eats a lot of food. The sun is hot and she is tired. Lucretia looks into the pyramid. She thinks; 'It's not hot in the pyramid. I want to go in the pyramid and sleep.'

'Stop!' shouts Anna. 'Stop!' shouts the director. 'Stop!' shouts the tall lady. But Lucretia does not stop. She runs quickly into the pyramid.

• What does the sign say?

Anna runs into the pyramid. She wants to find Lucretia, but there are four doors inside the pyramid and Anna does not know where to go next.

It is very dark and cold. She shivers. She is afraid of the dark.

The director comes into the pyramid. Anna is happy to see him. 'Which door?' she asks.

'I don't know,' says the director. 'But there's someone who does know.'

They go out. A man is working near the pyramid. Anna and the director tell him about Lucretia. They ask the man about the doors.

'Look at this,' the man says. He puts his hand in his pocket and takes out a map. It is very old. There are words and pictures on the map. 'Take this,' says the man. Anna and the director look at the map.

- Anna must go through one of the doors.
  Which colour is the door to the pyramid?

Anna runs into the pyramid and through the blue door. She is in a long room. Anna runs through another door and into another long room. The director and the man with the map run after her. They have a torch.

Anna calls, 'Lucretia! Lucretia! Where are you?' She listens but she cannot hear anything.

Anna walks carefully because it is dark. She hears a noise. 'Lucretia? Is that you, Lucretia?' Anna is afraid. She thinks, 'What's that noise?'

Then she hears the noise again. This time it is very close. 'Meow!'

'Oh, Lucretia! There you are. Come here.'

Suddenly there is a light. The man with the torch and the director come into the room. Lucretia does not like the torch. She runs away. Anna cannot see her in the dark. 'Lucretia, you bad cat!' she shouts.

Anna and the director come to a door. Anna hits the door but she cannot open it. The director sees some keys. 'One of these must open the door,' he says.

• Which key opens the door?

Anna opens the door with the key. The door opens very slowly. On the other side is a small room. There are a lot of things in the room and they are all gold! Nobody says anything for a long time.

Then they all walk slowly into the room. There is a statue of a cat. The director puts his hand on it and the statue says: 'Meow!' It is not a statue. It is Lucretia. The director, the man with the map, and Anna laugh.

• One of these things is not in the room. Which is it?

Anna comes out of the pyramid. She is carrying Lucretia. Her mother, Alberta, is waiting for her.

'Ah, there you are, Anna. And Lucretia! You're in an advertisement. How exciting!' Anna puts Lucretia down. 'Are you being good? Do you like my hair?'

The director says: 'They're being very good. Look!' He shows Alberta a gold necklace.

A little later, Alberta says to the director, 'We must go home now.' Alberta and Anna walk to the car. Alberta suddenly stops. 'Wait! Where's Lucretia?' she says. Everyone calls the cat but they cannot see her.

• Lucretia does not want to go home. Why not?

Glossary

advertisement a short film used to sell something

clap a noise when hands are hit together

film a story in the cinema or on television

follow stay close behind someone

food something you eat

gold an expensive metal

haircut a person has a haircut to make their hair shorter

holiday a time to rest. People often have a holiday in the summer

light something that helps you see in the dark

pick up to lift and hold

shiver a little shake. People shiver when they are cold or scared

shout to speak loudly

statue a piece of wood or metal cut to look like a person or animal

wipe to make clean

Answers to the puzzles

page 3
She goes into Curly's for a haircut.

page 5

page 7

page 9
He can't sit on his chair
because there is cat food
on it.

page 11
The man and the woman are
in the wrong places.

page 13
The sign says *Wipe your feet*.

page 15
The door is blue.

page 17

page 19
There is no telephone in the room
in the pyramid.

page 21

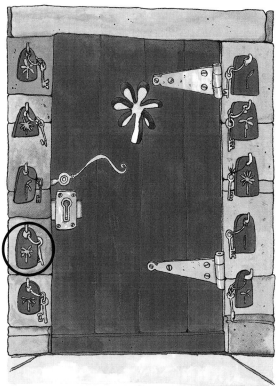

Oxford University Press, Great Clarendon Street, Oxford OX2 6DP

Oxford   New York

Athens   Auckland   Bangkok   Bogota   Bombay
Buenos Aires   Calcutta   Cape Town   Dar es Salaam
Delhi   Florence   Hong Kong   Istanbul   Karachi
Kuala Lumpur   Madras   Madrid   Melbourne
Mexico City   Nairobi   Paris   Singapore
Taipei   Tokyo   Toronto   Warsaw
and associated companies in
Berlin   Ibadan

OXFORD and OXFORD ENGLISH
are trade marks of Oxford University Press

ISBN 0 19 422506 2

© Oxford University Press

First published 1998

No unauthorized photocopying

Printed in Hong Kong